FRIENDS
OF ACPL

D1708853

DO NOT REMOVE
CARDS FROM POCKET

ALLEN COUNTY PUBLIC LIBRARY

FORT WAYNE, INDIANA 46802

You may return this book to any agency, branch,
or bookmobile of the Allen County Public Library.

7/89

What happens when you

EAT?

WHAT HAPPENS WHEN . . . ?

What Happens When You Breathe?
What Happens When You Catch a Cold?
What Happens When You Eat?
What Happens When You Grow?
What Happens When You Hurt Yourself?
What Happens When You Listen?
What Happens When You Look?
What Happens When You Run?
What Happens When You Sleep?
What Happens When You Talk?
What Happens When You Think?
What Happens When You Touch and Feel?

Library of Congress Cataloging-in-Publication Data

Richardson, Joy.
  What happens when you eat?

  (What happens when— ?)
  Bibliography: p.
  Includes index.
  Summary: Describes how our bodies process the food we eat and turn it into energy.
  1. Ingestion — Juvenile literature.   2. Digestion — Juvenile literature.
3. Metabolism — Juvenile literature.   [1. Digestion.   2. Metabolism]
I. Maclean, Colin, 1930-   ill.   II. Maclean, Moira, ill.   III. Title.
IV. Series: Richardson, Joy.   What happens when— ?
QP147.R53   1986   612'.3   86-3726

ISBN 1-55532-130-5
ISBN 1-55532-105-4 (lib. bdg.)

This North American edition first published in 1986 by
Gareth Stevens, Inc.
7317 West Green Tree Road   Milwaukee, Wisconsin 53223, USA

First published in the United Kingdom by Hamish Hamilton Children's Books with an original text copyright by Joy Richardson.

Typeset by Ries Graphics, ltd.
Series editor: MaryLee Knowlton
Cover design: Gary Moseley
Additional illustration/design: Laurie Shock

What happens when you
EAT?

Joy Richardson

pictures by
Colin and Moira Maclean

introduction by
Gail Zander, Ph.D.

Gareth Stevens Publishing
Milwaukee

. . . a note to parents and teachers

Curiosity about the body begins shortly after birth when babies explore with their mouths. Gradually children add to their knowledge through sight, sound, and touch. They ask questions. However, as they grow, confusion or shyness may keep them from asking questions, and they may acquire little knowledge about what lies beneath their skin. More than that, they may develop bad feelings about themselves based on ignorance or misinformation.

The *What Happens When . . . ?* series helps children learn about themselves in a way that promotes healthy attitudes about their bodies and how they work. They learn that their bodies are systems of parts that work together to help them grow, stay well, and function. Each book in the series explains and illustrates how one of the systems works.

With the understanding of how their bodies work, children learn the importance of good health habits. They learn to respect the wonders of the body. With knowledge and acceptance of their bodies' parts, locations, and functions, they can develop a healthy sense of self.

This attractive series of books is an invaluable source of information for children who want to learn clear, correct, and interesting facts about how their bodies work.

GAIL ZANDER, Ph.D.
CHILD PSYCHOLOGIST
MILWAUKEE PUBLIC SCHOOLS

Do you know what happens
when you eat
a crunchy apple,
some chewy meat,
an ice-cream cone,
or a sticky sweet?

Your front teeth bite the food.
Your tongue licks it.
Your back teeth chew it up.
Meat needs a lot of chewing.

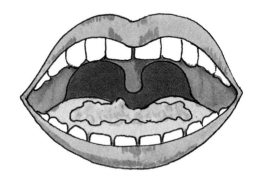

Think of something delicious to eat.
Is your mouth watering?
This is the saliva getting ready
for the food.

Saliva comes out
from under your tongue.
It makes the food soft and wet.
This makes it easier to chew.

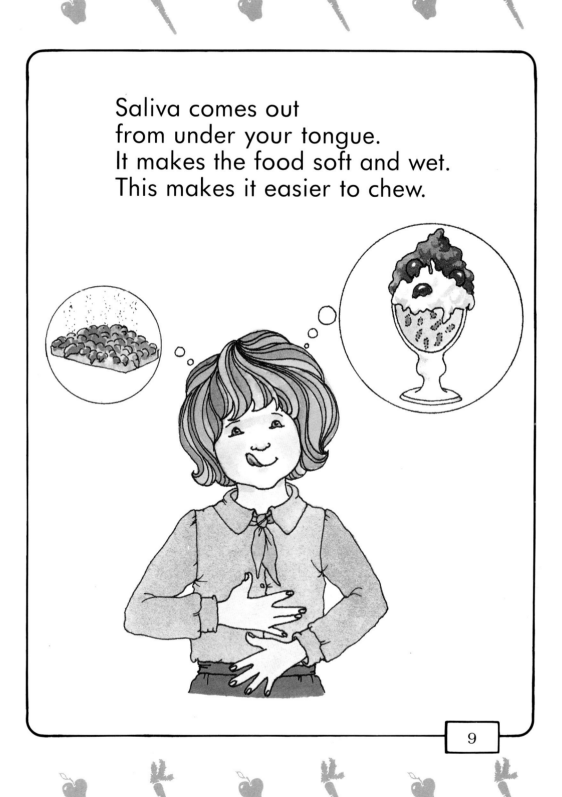

Look at your tongue in a mirror.
It is covered with little spots.
How many can you count?

Some of the spots help you taste things.
They are called taste buds.
Some taste buds taste sweet things.
Some taste buds taste bitter things.

Try tasting these foods on
the front and the back
and the side of your tongue.

jam   sugar   lemon   salt

Where are the best taste buds
for tasting each food?

You also taste food by its smell.
What happens if you hold your nose
when you are eating?

Your tongue pushes the food
to the back of your mouth.

In your throat there are two pipes.
One is for air and one is for food.

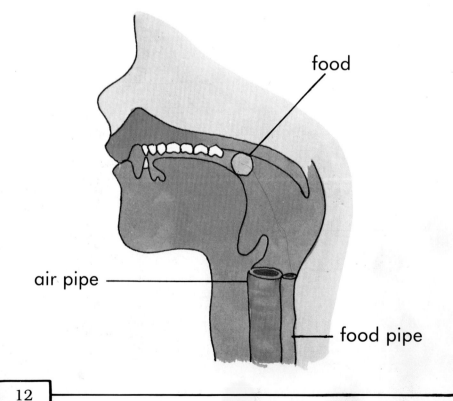

food

air pipe

food pipe

When you swallow,
the food is pushed into the food pipe.
The air pipe closes
to keep food out.
If food went down it, you would choke.

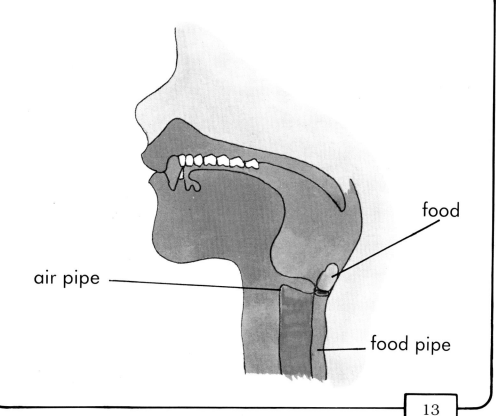

food

air pipe

food pipe

The food pipe has elastic sides.
They push the food down
to your stomach.

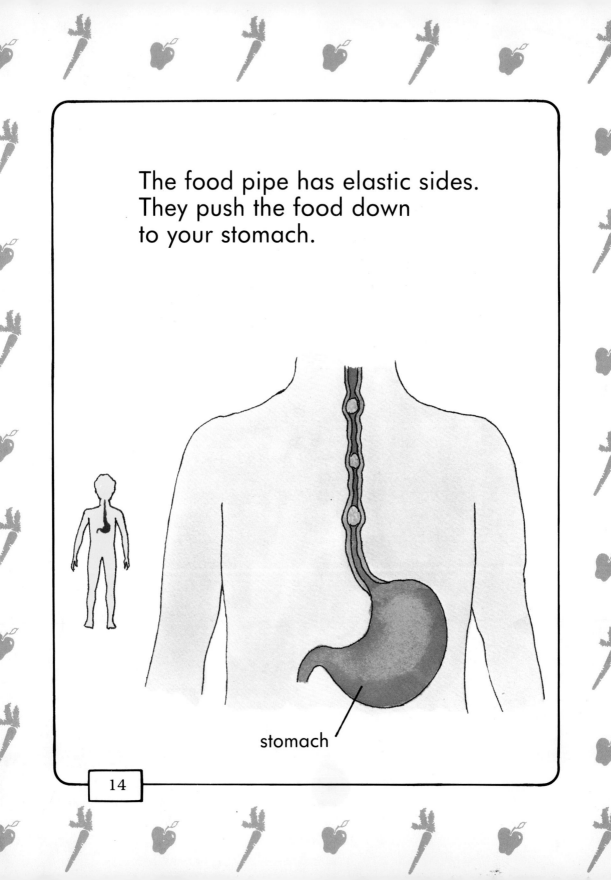

stomach

Blow a little air into a long balloon.
Tie the end tightly.
Use your hands to squeeze the air
slowly along the balloon.
Your food pipe takes food to your
stomach like this — even if you are
upside down!

Strong muscles in the walls
of your stomach churn the food around.

Your stomach can change shape.
It gets fatter when there is
a lot of food in it.

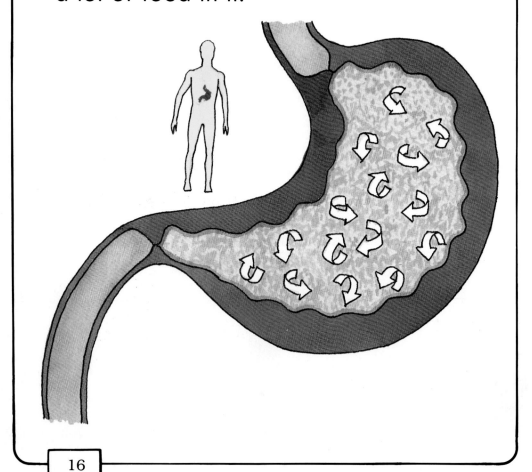

Juices from the stomach walls
mix with the food and break it up.
When it gets soft, like oatmeal,
a hole opens to let it out.

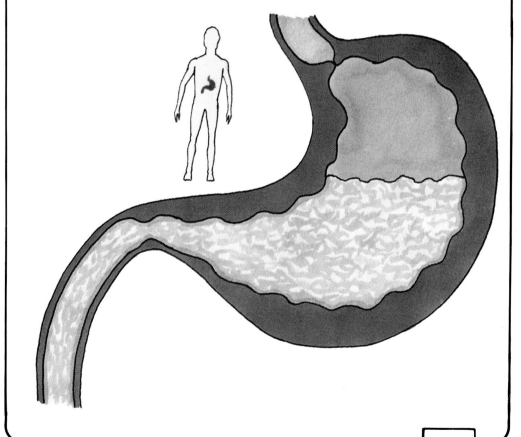

The food goes into a long, thin tube
and then into a fatter tube.
These tubes are called intestines.
They are folded up inside you.

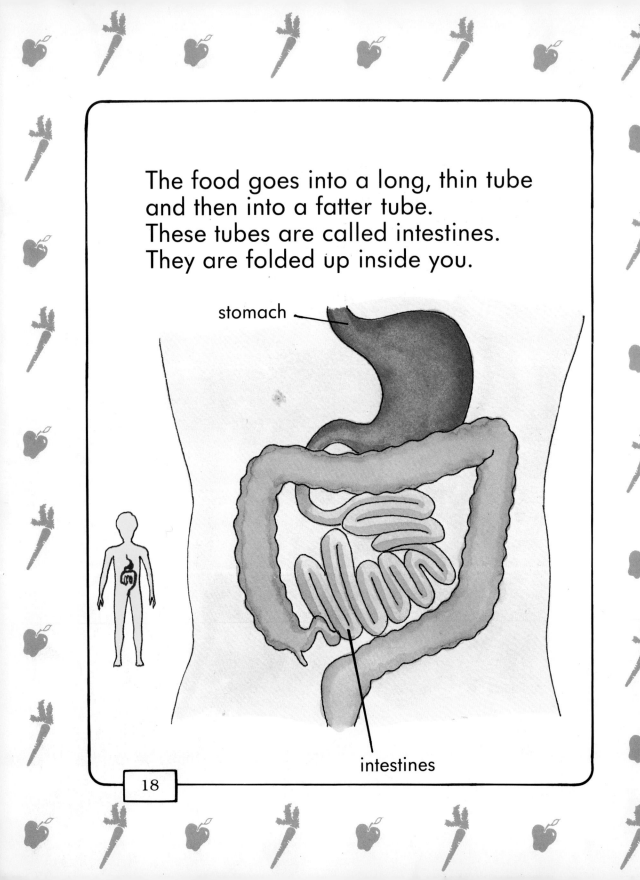

stomach

intestines

Your intestines will grow to be about 24 feet long.
How far would they stretch if you could take them out?

Cut a 24 foot length of string.
Can you fold it to fit on this page?

The food moves slowly
along the intestines.
More juices are needed to help digest
the food and get all the goodness out.
The food is very watery now.

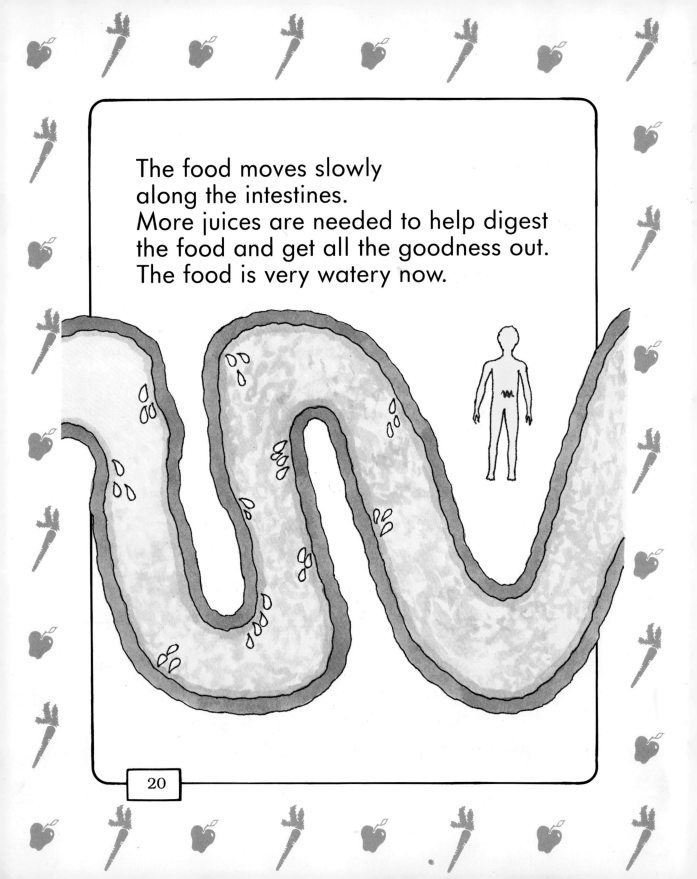

Put these foods into bowls:
    a slice of bread,
    a piece of apple,
    a cookie,
    a spoonful of butter.

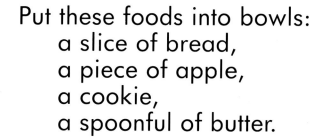
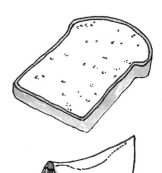

Add three tablespoons of water.
Mash them up with a knife and fork.
Which foods break up most easily?

Some foods need special juices
to break them up as they go along
the intestines.

21

Inside the intestines,
the walls are very wrinkled.
The goodness in the watery food
is sucked up.
It mixes with your blood.

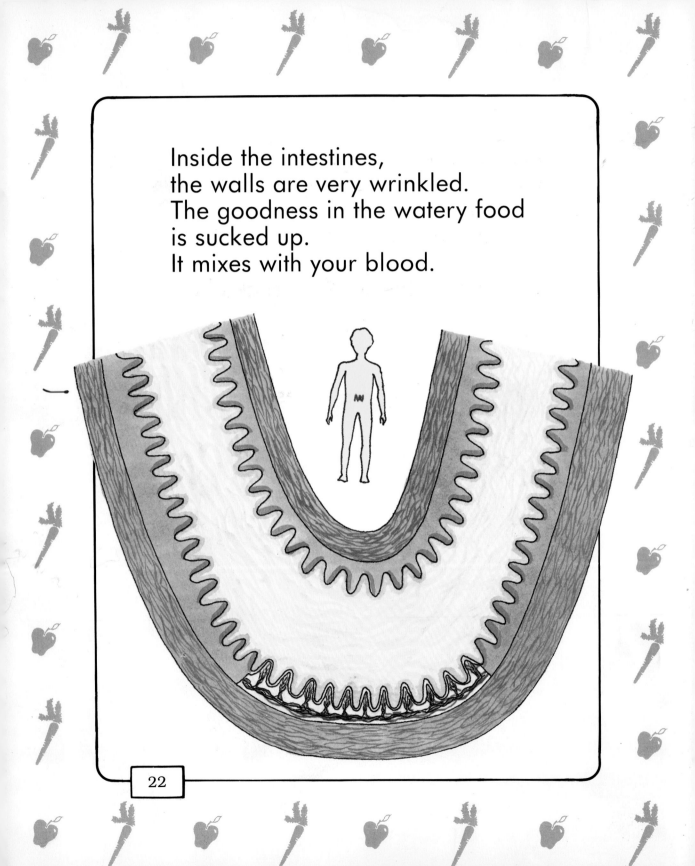

Put some water in a tray.
Dip some strips of paper towel
or some pieces of sponge
into the water.

Watch how the water is sucked up.

The goodness in the watery food
is sucked up into your blood through
the wrinkles in your intestines.

The blood goes along thin tubes to
every part of your body.
The food goes with it.
It gives you energy.

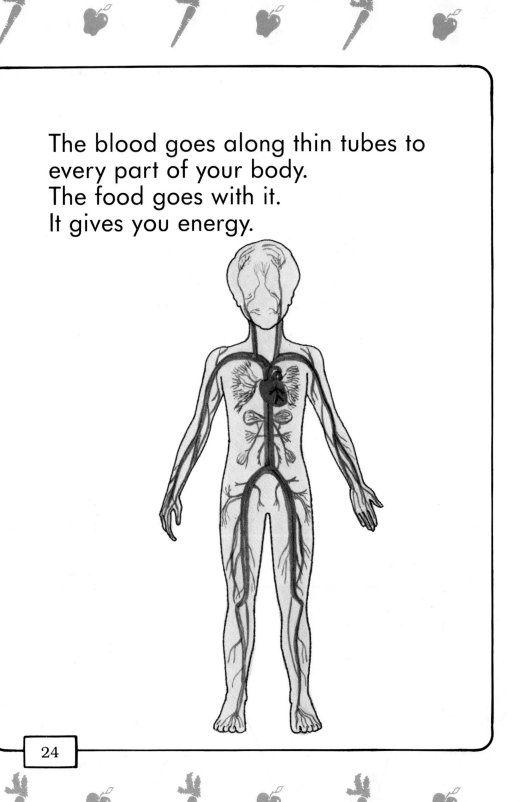

You need energy for
        running,
        breathing,
        thinking,
        talking,
and everything else you do.
A car needs fuel to make it go.
You need food to keep you going.

Some food is not needed.
It stays behind in your intestines.
It is quite dry now.
It goes on down to the end.

You push it out
when you go to the toilet.

If you eat lunch
at 12 o'clock,

by 2 o'clock your stomach
is nearly empty.

At bedtime, some food
is still in your intestines.

During the night, your
blood carries the food
around your body.

Right now,
your body is busy
digesting what you
have eaten today!

Do you know where to find your

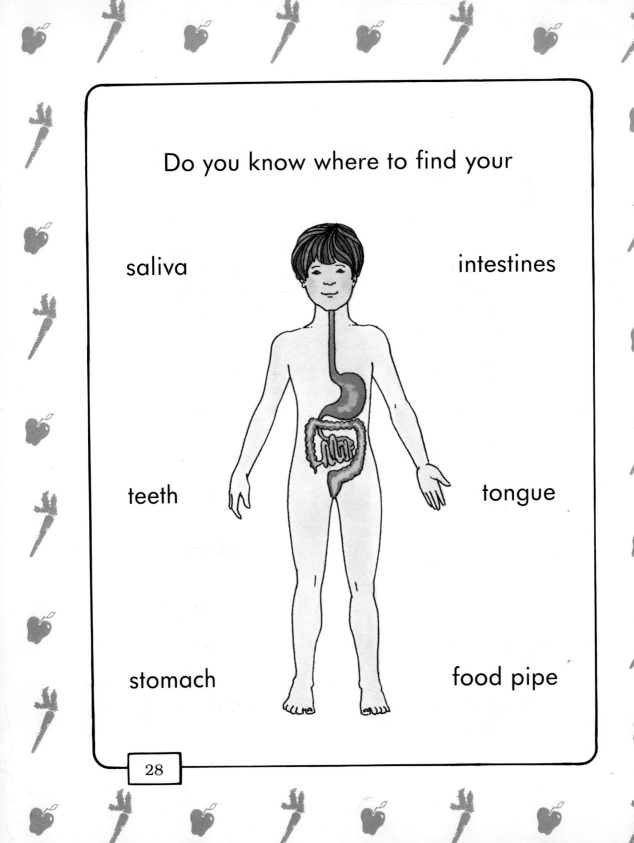

saliva

intestines

teeth

tongue

stomach

food pipe

How Does That Happen?

Did you find all these things to do in *What Happens When You EAT?* If not, turn back to the pages listed here and have some fun seeing how your body works.

1. Make your mouth water. (page 9)

2. Count the spots on your tongue. (page 10)

3. Practice tasting. (page 11)

4. See how a balloon is like your food pipe. (page 15)

5. Check out the length of your intestines. (page 19)

6. What foods break up most easily? (page 21)

7. Use sponges to see how the intestines work. (page 23)

8. Find the parts of your body that digest food. (page 28)

More Books About Eating

Listed below are more books about what happens when you eat. If you are interested in them, check your library or bookstore.

Beginning to Learn about Tasting. Allington/Cowles (Raintree)

Fat and Skinny. Balestrino (Crowell)

Food, Nutrition, and You. Peary/Smith (Scribner's)

From Head to Toes: How Your Body Works. Packard (Simon & Schuster)

Getting Ready to Cook (First Cookbook Library). de Villiers/van der Berg (Gareth Stevens)

How Do We Smell? Blakely (Creative Education)

It's Fun to Cook. Fellows (Gareth Stevens)

Junk Food — What It Is, What It Does. Seixas (Greenwillow)

Nutrition: A New True Book. LeMaster (Childrens Press)

A Tasting Party. Moncure (Childrens Press)

Vitamins — What They Are, What They Do. Seixas (Greenwillow)

What Happens to a Hamburger. Showers (Harper & Row/Crowell)

Why Do We Eat? Elspeland (Creative Education)

Your Weight. Eagles (Franklin Watts)

Where to Find More About Eating

Here are some people you can write away to for more information about what happens when you eat. Be sure to tell them exactly what you want to know about. Include your full name and address so they can write back to you.

Gerber Products Company
Fremont, Michigan 49412

Public Affairs Pamphlets
381 Park Avenue South
New York, New York 10016

Index